Dear George

GEORGE BURNS

Dear George

Advice & Answers From America's Leading Expert on Everything From A to B

G. P. PUTNAM'S SONS

NEW YORK

G. P. Putnam's Sons
Publishers Since 1838
200 Madison Avenue
New York, NY 10016

The author gratefully acknowledges permission from
Fisher Music Corp. to quote lyrics from "She Looks Like
Helen Brown" by Fred Fisher and Billy Rose, © 1936
Fisher Music Corp.
Photographs © 1985 by Peter Borsari
unless otherwise indicated.

Library of Congress Cataloging in Publication Data

Burns, George, date.
Dear George.

1. American wit and humor.   I. Title.
PN6162.B824   1985   816'.54   85-12312
ISBN 0-399-13105-1

Book design by Joe Marc Freedman
Printed in the United States of America
1   2   3   4   5   6   7   8   9   10

Contents

Dear George

Introduction

Dear Reader—

Wait a minute, that doesn't sound very positive.
Dear Readers—

Yeah, that looks better. You weren't expecting another book, were you. Neither was I. Let me tell you how it happened. A few days ago I was busy sitting in my office blowing smoke rings when the phone rang. It was Phyllis Grann, my editor and publisher at Putnam's, calling from New York to tell me how great my last book was doing.

"Do you realize," she said, "that *Dr. Burns' Prescription for Happiness* has been on the *New York Times* Best Seller list for eighteen straight weeks?"

I said I didn't believe it. She said neither did the *New York Times*, but we had to face it, I was a smash and when could she have my next book.

I told her to forget it. In the first place, I wouldn't know what to write about, and in the second place, I was too busy to do another book. "Look, I don't sit around here blowing smoke rings. I've got a TV special to do, concerts, personal appearances at Caesars Vegas, Tahoe and Atlantic City, and on top of that I'm reading a script for a new movie. I play this old detective who's retired, and I'm sitting around the park—"

"George," she interrupted, "I'd love to hear the plot, but I'm not taking no for an answer on the book. You've got two best sellers in a row. You're hot!"

"I'm hot?" I said. "Tell that to Trixie Hicks and Elsie Huber and Lily Delight." I waited for the laugh. Nothing. I tried again. "I'm hot? Tell that to my hands and feet. I wear gloves and socks in the steam room." Nothing again. "I'm hot? Tell that to—" I would have gone on but the operator cut us off.

However, Phyllis wasn't through. For the next three days I got big bouquets of flowers from her. And on the fourth day she was back on the phone.

"Phyllis," I said, "I love you, I love Putnam's, I love the *New York Times*, but the book is out. And stop with the flowers. At my age flowers scare me."

She started to laugh. "And laughing at that lousy joke won't do you any good, either," I said, "because I can't even see across my desk it's piled so high with letters that I can't find time to answer."

"That's it! That's it!" she shrieked. "I knew you'd come up with it!"

"What did I come up with?"

"The book! Letters from people who write you their problems and want your advice!"

"I just came up with that, huh?"

"You're a genius. I love it! Now if we can just think of a great title!"

"Hold it," I said. "You mean I'm supposed to come up with answers for all those people?"

"George, with that storehouse of wit and wisdom you have to draw from it'll be a breeze."

"But, Phyllis, giving advice—that's not for me. That's for 'Dear Abby.' "

"That's it!! That's it!!!"

"What's it?" I asked, switching the receiver to my other ear. (I didn't really do that, but it's nice writing. It sort of livens up the dialogue.)

"You got it, George! That's the title!"

"I did it again, huh? Okay, we'll call my book *Dear Abby*."

"No, no, no, it's *Dear George*! It can't miss!"

I said, "Good. I came up with the book and I came up with the title, now here's my first letter: 'Dear Phyllis— I can't do the book, I'm too busy.' "

"George," she whispered, "I'll give you twice what you got last time."

"Another letter: 'Dear Phyllis— I'll do the book.' "

Okay, so I was an author again. *Dear George* would be the sixth book I've written, which isn't bad for a guy who has only read two.

But after we hung up, I started thinking. What have I got myself into? Can I do it? Am I qualified to answer all those letters? It's true I have a storehouse of wit and wisdom to draw from, but I've been drawing on that storehouse for 89 years. It could be overdrawn.

I must be crazy. How can I do a book when I've got all these other things going on? But I said I'll do it, and when I say I'll do it, I do it! I haven't gone back on my word for the last three weeks.

Look, something will just have to go. What can I do, I'll give up my Tuesday-night bowling.

Author getting started.

1

The First Ten Letters

Dear George—

My boyfriend and I have never made love with the light on. I'm dying to try it and see what it's like. Do you think this is an unreasonable desire?

Pittsburgh Penny

Dear Pitts—

There's nothing wrong with making love with the light on. Just make sure the car door is closed.

.　　.　　.

Dear George—

Now that I'm getting up in years, my doctor keeps warning me to keep my weight down and eat the right foods. But who knows what's right to eat anymore? What do you think about all those natural food and high-fiber diets I'm always hearing about?

Aging Gracefully

Dear Aging—

I personally stay away from natural foods. At my age I need all the preservatives I can get. On the other hand, what could be wrong with a high-fiber diet? When was the last time you saw a fat moth?

Dear George—

My wife, who I loved and miss very much, passed away three weeks ago, and I have yearnings for the opposite sex again. I'd like to do something about it, but my kids say it's too soon. Actually, it's been three weeks and two days. I want to do the right thing, but how long does a man have to wait for sex after his wife dies?

Bereaved Husband

Dear Bereaved—

I'd say it depends on how long you had to wait for it when your wife was alive.

(This letter may seem like an exaggeration, but people are strange. Let me tell you what really happened to me one time. I was coming out of the Palace Theater Building and I ran into this actor I knew. He said, "George, I've got a big problem. My wife passed away, and there's this gorgeous tomato who wants to have an affair with me."

I said, "When did your wife die, Jim?" and he said, "Yesterday."

I couldn't believe my ears. I said, "How could you think of having an affair if your wife passed away yesterday?" and he said, "That's the problem, I'd have to miss the funeral.")

Dear George—

I'm involved with a much younger woman, but my mother doesn't approve. She says younger women are only out for one thing. I love my mother, but I think she's all wrong on this. Don't you?

Good Son

Dear Good—

I'm not sure what your mother is referring to. I'm taking out a young woman tonight, and I know what she's out for—a good meal. What she's in for remains to be seen.

.   .   .

Dear George—

Last night I had a blind date with a wealthy doctor that my parents fixed up for me. He was nice, but ugly. Honest, George, he looked like a gorilla. I really believe I have found the missing link, and what's worse, he wants to go out with me again. My parents want me to marry him, and I know he would. But how could I eat breakfast every morning with that hideous monkey sitting across the table from me?

Apprehensive

Dear App—

He's wealthy, he's a doctor, marry him, skip breakfast and eat a big lunch.

P.S. Let me know when you get married and I'll send you some peanuts.

This is what I have breakfast with every morning. And she's complaining.

Dear George—

We're a young married couple considering starting a family. How far apart do you think children should be spaced?

Anxious to Get Started

Dear Anxious—

About five miles.

.   .   .

Dear George—

My fiancé dresses like Boy George, talks like Michael Jackson, but looks like Willie Nelson and walks like John Wayne. We're spending our honeymoon at Caesars Palace. Do you have any advice?

Engaged

Dear Engaged—

Ask for group rates.

(I'm glad they're going to Caesars Palace. It's my favorite hotel, I play there all the time. Last time I played there I caught Tom Jones. He was working across the street. Women love him. During his act they throw their room keys up on the stage. They throw their room keys at me, too, but after they check out.)

Dear George—

I am a high school junior, and I'm in love with this girl in my French class. How can I tell if this is the real thing or just puppy love?

High School Hector

Dear High—

Feel your nose. If it's cold and it's damp, then it's just puppy love. Try not to soil the rug while you're getting over it.

.   .   .

Dear George—

My marriage is just about on the rocks. The problem is that my husband and I don't know what to do about it. Should we take a vacation and try to put the marriage back together, or get a divorce and go our separate ways?

Up in the Air

Dear Up—

I don't know why you're having a problem deciding. It's simple. When a vacation is over, it's over. But a divorce is something you'll have forever.

Dear George—

I need therapy, but I'm a little suspicious of the psychiatrist who was recommended to me. I found out that instead of a couch he has a big double bed in his office. Should I go to him or not?

Paranoid

Dear Par—

Go to him. Why would a double bed make you suspicious? Maybe he likes to take a nap between patients. Maybe he's got a bad back. Maybe his nurse has a bad back. If you don't have faith in people, kid, you'll never get well.

(I've never gone to a psychiatrist, but I play bridge with one two or three times a week. One day I said to him, "Al, how can you stand that work of yours? How can you listen to people's problems eight hours a day?" He said, "Who listens?" Now I know why he's such a lousy bridge player.)

END OF CHAPTER

Author beginning to make headway.

Dear George—

I love the material so far. Keep it up. Just one little thought. In your introduction you write, *"Dear George* would be the sixth book I've written, which isn't bad for a guy who has only read two."

Very funny, but if memory serves, you did that same gag about your last book.

Phyllis

Dear Phyllis—

Glad you like the stuff. However, on your little thought, memory doesn't serve you, because in the first place I didn't say it about my last book, I said it about *How to Live to Be 100—Or More.* And what I said was, "This is the fourth book I've written, which isn't bad for a guy who's only read two."

How is that the same? One is the sixth book, the other was the fourth book—that's a whole different joke. I'd never do the same joke twice.

You have to assemble the right secretarial staff. It could be a long project.

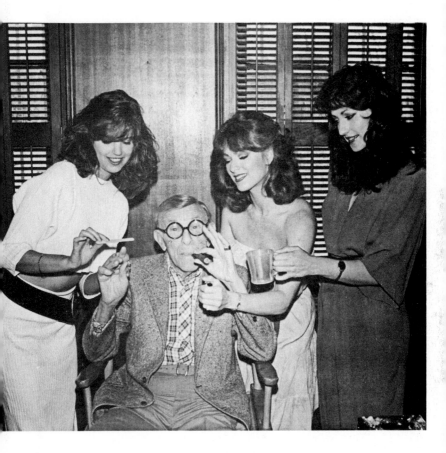

And they take shorthand, too.

2

The Second Ten Letters

Dear George—

I'm 72 and a widower who is just getting back into the dating game. So far I've had some very nice evenings with girls in their twenties and thirties. But I've been told they're too young for me. So I thought I'd get it straight from the horse's mouth. Do you think I should date these young girls, or should I stick to women my age?

Puzzled

Dear Puzzled—

The mouth isn't the part of the horse I'm used to being associated with, but as to your question, I would definitely advise you to stick to women your age. That will leave more of the young ones for me.

Of course, age isn't everything. I'd even take a smart, beautiful, 25-year-old over a dumb, homely kid who's 23. I'm very flexible.

Dear George—

I'm addicted to gambling. I'll bet on anything, and I've lost more money than I can count. I want to have a normal life, settle down and have a family, but I can't stop gambling long enough to do that.

Crapped Out

Dear Crapped—

Get married. The odds on winning aren't any better. You'll still have a lot of bad nights, but if it doesn't work out, your wife can only get half of what you started with.

.　.　.

Dear George—

If good girls go to heaven, where do bad girls go?

Little Joe

Dear Little—

Anywhere they want.

(If I'm not mistaken, Mae West answered that question the same way. Mae and I had the same sense of humor, but different deliveries. With that way of speaking she had, Mae could make anything sound naughty. One time she ran into Gracie in Beverly Hills, and said, "How's George?" Gracie came home and wanted to divorce me.)

Dear George—

I'm very superstitious. I don't walk under ladders or cross paths of black cats. And I don't get out of bed on Friday the 13th. But what about holidays? I heard it brings bad luck to have sex on Ground Hog Day.

Worried

Dear Worried—

Don't worry. Unless you're planning to have it with a ground hog. And it would probably be bad luck only for the ground hog.

(Some people worry about everything. Not me, I never worry. If I have a problem, I don't take it to bed with me, I tell her to go home.)

Dear George—

My wife has a fantastic job, and while she's away at work all day I'm home doing the housework and taking care of our three small children. Do you think this could confuse our kids about the mother-father roles, and if so, would that be harmful in later years?

Stay-at-Home Father

Dear Stay-At—

What you're saying is that your wife brings home the bacon and you cook it. I hear lots of talk these days about the effects of this kind of situation, and for every expert who says it's bad, it seems there's another who thinks it's good. All I know is that when I was growing up I had no trouble telling my father from my mother. He was the one with the beard, and she was the one with the mustache. Or was it the other way around? Wait, now I remember. My father had a beard, but it was my sister Goldie who had the mustache. We used to tell her to shave it off like mother did.

(Actually, my mother didn't have a mustache, my sister didn't have a mustache, and neither did I. My father did have a beard, but if I just mentioned that, it would be a pretty dull answer. Did my father have a beard! It ran from the third floor down to the street. I never had to use the stairs, I used to shinny down his beard.

Look, I like to throw in little things like this from time to time. It breaks the monotony—not yours, mine.)

. . .

Dear George—

I'm very nearsighted, and I have learned that men don't make passes at girls who wear glasses. Yesterday I was walking along the beach in my bikini and took off my glasses. I couldn't tell if anybody made a pass at me or not, I couldn't see anything. What am I to do?

Out of Focus

Dear Focus—

Put on your glasses and take off your bikini. Or better yet, take off your glasses and your bikini. But you might catch cold, so you better wear a hat.

I like girls with glasses—especially if one is for me.

Dear George—

I seem to be having a hard time getting ahead in life. The other day I read that Thomas Edison once said, "Genius is 1% inspiration and 99% perspiration." Do you believe that?

Going Nowhere

Dear Going—

I'm not sure Edison ever said that. All I know is the last time I danced with him he could have used a can of Right Guard.

(That really deserves a better answer. To me, Genius is 1% inspiration and 99% good writers. I don't sweat.)

. . .

Dear George—

I'm in love with a wonderful girl, but she happens to be a professional. And I don't mean a dancer, I'm talking about the oldest profession. This worries me. Do you think I should marry her?

Unsigned

Dear Un—

Of course. She'll make you a rich man. She'll be saving you $200 a night. At the end of the year you'll be worth a fortune.

(These days it's not easy to tell a professional girl from a Vassar graduate. Come to think of it, it never was easy. I remember years ago Georgie Jessel and I were playing the B. F. Keith Theater in Philadelphia, and he couldn't stop bragging about this high-class girl he spent the night with in Cleveland. He said, "What a lady. She knows absolutely nothing about vaudeville. Her world is culture. All she can talk about is the opera, the ballet, the symphony, great works of art."

A week later he got a call from her, and she said, "Georgie, I've got bad news for you. You gave me Cupid's eczema."

Jessel said, "Wait a minute, I just came from the doctor. I didn't give it to you, you gave it to me."

"Oh," she said, "then the Three Stanley Brothers gave it to me.")

Dear George—

I own a good business, have a nice home and a wife whom I dearly love. But she always wants to have her way. And she has a habit that really bugs me. She always reminds me way ahead of time when her birthday is coming. And then she tells me exactly what she wants. Like this birthday she told me she wants a red convertible with white leather.

Before she even brought it up I was already thinking about getting her a car, but I had my eye on a snazzy, dark blue convertible. She takes the whole kick out of it for me. How can I explain that to her?

Farley in Fairfield

Dear Farley—

Don't explain. Give her what you want to give her. It's your gift. You have to start taking charge. Women like that. That's why he-men types like Gable, John Wayne, Clint Eastwood and the rest of us stay popular.

Dear George—

My boyfriend is a rock fan, but it's not what you'd think. I don't mean Mick Jagger or Rod Stewart. He loves to go rock climbing, and that's where we go on our dates, to different rock cliffs. When we get home he's always too pooped to make love. I just bought a new, extra, extra firm bed, and even that doesn't help. What should I do?

Upset

Dear Up—

Sorry, kid, it sounds like you're caught between a rock and a hard place.

(Some of you probably think I'm making up these letters just so I can have funny answers. I'm surprised at you, thinking a thing like that! I'm a nice, quiet, soft-spoken, 89-year-old man. I played "God"—three times—without makeup. And I got paid—three times. Making up letters! My older brother would be ashamed of me if I did a thing like that!)

END OF CHAPTER

Author making real progress.

3

Some
Interesting
Letters

Dear George—

I've been trying to score with this gorgeous girl at work for over a year. But every time I try a squeeze play she's got some left-field excuse. I can't get to first base with her. It's not that I haven't tried. I keep coming up to bat, but I'm always striking out. I'm beginning to think it's time for a pinch hitter. If you're interested, I'll be happy to send you her phone number.

Bench Warmer

Dear Bench—

Don't bother. The season's over for me.

.   .   .

Dear George—

Last night my husband and I went to a masquerade party, and I went as a man and he went as a woman. And with my dress, blonde wig and makeup he looked very attractive. In fact, one fellow danced with him practically the whole night, and they ended up leaving together. Should I be worried?

Having Second Thoughts

Dear Having—

Only if you need the dress back by Tuesday.

(This reminds me of an incident that happened once with my close friend Jack Benny. We had to do a benefit performance, and I talked Jack into doing a Burns & Allen routine where he played Gracie. Now when Jack did something he went all out. He wouldn't play a woman like Milton Berle. He got hold of the dress Rita Hayworth wore in Gilda, *which fitted him like a glove, put on a beautiful black wig and even wore a garter belt and shaved his legs. He was a doll and the routine was a riot.*

After the show I went to his dressing room, and before I could congratulate him he started screaming. I said, "What are you so upset about?" He said, "I'll tell you what I'm upset about! When I was walking down the hall three guys whistled at me, that's why I'm upset!"

I said, "Jack, you've got beautiful legs." "Don't try to make up to me," he said. "I should never have let you talk me into this. It's embarrassing, it's humiliating!" And he stomped out of the dressing room.

Jack was my friend, now I was upset. I didn't know what to do. Finally, two days later I went over to his house to apologize for having him wear that outfit. And when he opened the door he was still in it. I didn't know whether to apologize or kiss him. So I did both.)

That's right, he shaved his legs.

47

Dear George—

My wife keeps nagging me that it's time for me to have a talk with my 12-year-old son and tell him about the birds and the bees. To me he is still a little boy, and I feel awkward discussing this subject with him. What would you advise?

Reluctant

Dear Re—

Do what my father did when my mother nagged him to tell me about the birds and the bees. He took me to Coney Island, pointed to a couple making love under the boardwalk and said, "Your mother wants you to know that the birds and the bees do the same thing."

Dear George—

Now that I'm getting older, more and more of my friends are passing away, and I'm expected to go to each and every one of their funerals. But I really hate funerals. Am I wrong for not wanting to attend these depressing events?

Grave Situation

Dear Grave—

Just remember, if you don't go to their funerals, they won't come to yours.

Dear George—

My Uncle Jake recently died. After his funeral the family all gathered at my cousin's house to pay their respects. They not only had a catered buffet, but there in the middle of the table was a replica of Uncle Jake done in chopped liver. I found it tasteless and totally abhorrent. Don't you agree?

In from Outta Town

Dear In from Outta—

I agree. There's nothing worse than tasteless chopped liver.

(That letter's like the story about old Sam who is passing away at home in his bed. The family is all gathered around, and in the middle of his good-byes this wonderful aroma hits him.

"Becky," he says, "isn't that chopped liver I smell?"

She says, "Yes, Sam, it is."

And he says, "Becky, one last time I gotta have some of your chopped liver."

And she says, "You can't, it's for after."

I would have included this story in my letter to In from Outta, but she might have found it taste-less.)

Dear George—

My best friend has a dog who is very ill, and my friend tells me she is planning a big funeral, with a casket, services, eulogies and the whole bit. This seems a little eerie to me, but I suppose I'll have to attend. Am I also expected to send flowers?

Friend's Next-Best Friend

Dear Next-Best—

Yes, and a contribution to the dog's favorite charity.

(People get attached to their pets. I know a woman who had a fancier funeral for her poodle than for her husband.

And when Harpo Marx's cat passed away, he got George Jessel to do the eulogy. Jessel was never better. There wasn't a dry eye in the house as he eloquently recalled the deceased's loyalty, devotion and quiet generosity. But I thought he went a little too far when he said, "It would put you to shame if you knew what this cat did for Israel.")

With the King of Eulogies. I didn't like the way he was looking at me.

Dear George—

I've got a new boyfriend. Neither of us is talking marriage, but things are going so great it scares me. What could ruin a casual affair?

Fingers Crossed

Dear Fingers—

You're writing to the wrong adviser. I've never had a casual affair. I don't believe in casual affairs, I'm very formal. I even wear spats and a tie when I take a shower.

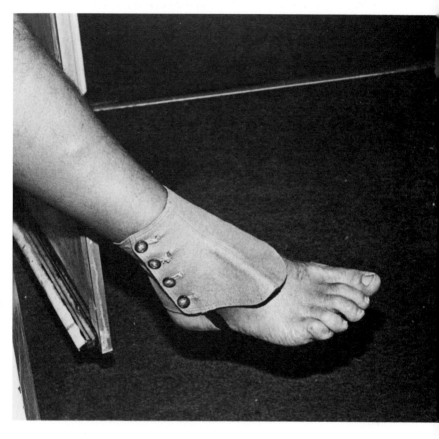

And you thought I just said that for a laugh.

Dear George—

I've got a good business, a nice home, a lovely wife and wonderful kids, but I'm a compulsive liar. I lie to everybody about everything, and it's really bothering me. How can I change?

Two-Faced

Dear Two—

I don't know quite what to say here. If you're lying about your business, home, wife and kids, you've got to change. But if you're not, keep lying.

. . .

Dear George—

My husband is constantly humiliating me in public about my size. Like if I have a cold, he'll say, "Look at her, the elephant's trunk is all stopped up." The other night when somebody asked what he was giving me for my birthday, he said, "A cowbell to wear around her neck so I'll know where she is." This really bothers me. Am I oversensitive?

Feeling Hurt

Dear Feeling—

You're not oversensitive, you're overweight. You should do something about it. If you want to lose 170 pounds right away, get rid of that rude husband of yours.

(I never had a weight problem. Nobody in my family did. We were seven sisters and five brothers, we were too poor to be fat. Our big Sunday-night dinner was bread and gravy. And you had to be very careful not to get your fingers in the gravy or somebody would eat them. To this day my brother Willy can't thumb a ride.)

. . .

Dear George—

I got your advice. And I almost bought the blue convertible for my wife's birthday, but I couldn't quite bring myself to do it. Are you sure about this? What if she really gets upset?

Farley in Fairfield

Dear Farley—

Stop worrying. Just get her what you want to get her. She'll respect you more for it. Trust me. I've been around for a while. When I was a boy the Dead Sea was only sick.

END OF CHAPTER

Author getting away from secretary. You don't believe it? Then how about the next one?

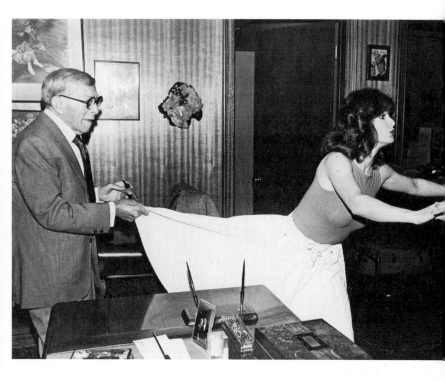

Secretary getting away from author.

4

More Interesting Letters

Dear George—

The entire staff of *The Playboy Advisor* department wishes you success in your new field of endeavor and would like to contribute some information that might be helpful. From past experience we have found that over ninety percent of the problems presented to us by people writing in letters are related to sex. These letters contain the usage of many words and expressions that may be unfamiliar to you because of the tremendous generation gap between you and anyone who is still living.

Therefore, we are enclosing, under separate cover, a complete glossary of such words and expressions in alphabetical order, ranging all the way from "Amoral" to "Zipper Ripper." You will find certain words and phrases have taken on an entirely new meaning from the way a man of your age might interpret them.

For example:

"Getting off" no longer means stepping out of a stagecoach.

"Making out" does not mean hitting a pop fly to the shortstop.

"S and M" does not stand for the dancing vaudeville team of Smith & Mahoney.

"T and A" is not the logo of the defunct railroad line that once operated between Tennessee and Alabama.

"Doing a trick" is not pulling a rabbit out of a hat.

A man referred to as "well-endowed" does not mean his family left him a lot of money.

Best wishes, and we hope our glossary will be of help to you.

Playboy Advisor Staff

Dear Advisor Staff—

Thanks for trying to update my thinking, but I happen to be hip to what's going down these days. It may surprise you, but I know that a "boob" is not a cartoon character named McNutt. And I am also aware that "buns" are not something you fondle while marketing to see if they're fresh. (Although I've been slapped in several stores for trying it.)

P.S. I'd read your magazine more often, but my glasses keep steaming over.

Dear George—

My husband and I find that variety is the spice of marriage. But after three years we're running out of places to make love. We've tried the park, the car, restaurants, trains, hot tubs, even furniture store displays. Can you think of any other real good place for us to try it?

Panting in Pittsburgh

Dear Panting—

Your bedroom. On second thought, you kids are killing yourselves. You don't need any new places, you should rest for an hour.

Dear George—

I'm getting up there in years, but I still like to play tennis with the guys, dance with the gals and have a few snorts with both. But everyone says I should slow down and act my age. As one geriatric to another, maybe you can tell me—at what point does one graduate from *elderly* to *old?*

Another Geriatric

Dear Geri—

You'll know you're *old* when everything hurts, and what doesn't hurt, doesn't work; when you feel like the night after and you haven't been anywhere; when you get winded playing chess; when your favorite part of the newspaper is "25 Years Ago Today"; when you're still chasing women, but can't remember why; when you stoop to tie your shoelaces and ask yourself, "What else can I do while I'm down here?"; when everybody goes to your birthday party and stands around the cake just to get warm.

(These things really happen when you get old. I know, because that's what my father keeps telling me.)

Dear George—

You amaze me. Everywhere I look, there you are—TV shows, commercials, nightclubs, movies. At your age, how do you keep it up?

Flabbergasted

Dear Flabber—

My manager, Irving Fein, helps me.

.　　.　　.

Dear George—

We watch you all the time here at the Home. You're our very favorite. You always seem so chipper and full of pep. But just between you, me and my pacemaker, how does it really feel to be 89?

Can Keep a Secret

(What do they want from me? That's three of these letters in a row. That's all I hear—old, old, old! So I'm too old to win a Charleston contest! They don't even have Charleston contests anymore! Who cares? So I'm 89, what's the big deal?! I'm not even going to answer this, one of my secretaries can do it!)

Dear Can Keep a Secret—

Mr. Burns wants me to answer you. As his secretary I can assure you that day in and day

65

out, no one feels better than he does. Or more often.

Black and Blue

(She's too funny. That's the last time she'll answer a letter for me.)

. . .

Dear George—

I'm 28 years old, and I must be attractive because I seem to turn guys on. The problem is they do the same thing for me—morning, noon and night. In high school I was known as Nina the Nympho. And it's not getting any better. If I'm with a man five minutes, I just can't control myself. I don't know what to do. Do you have any ideas?

In High Gear

Dear In High—

As a matter of fact I do have some ideas. But it's difficult going into them through the mail. However, I'm home after 8:00 P.M., Tuesdays and Thursdays, if you'd care to discuss your problem further.

P.S. Better make that Thursday. My couple is off that night, so we could really concentrate on the matter.

Thursday afternoon—author waving goodbye to his couple.

Thursday night—waiting for consultation.

Friday morning—exhausted from previous night's consultation.

Dear George—

When my husband and I got married I thought we'd be a very happy couple. Now that the honeymoon is over I realize he's not interested in the things I like to do, and I'm not interested in the things he likes to do. Is our marriage doomed?

Working At It

Dear Work—

Not necessarily. The fact that both of you are not interested in things the other one likes proves that you *do* have something in common. And that's a good beginning. Just be careful not to pressure one another into doing something you both like to do.

I suggest you find things neither of you like to do, and spend as much time as possible doing them together. For instance, not watching television together can be most enjoyable. And if you want a good, long, happy marriage, why don't you consider living in different towns together.

. . .

Dear George—

Maybe you can help. I'm in a quandary. Providing that an object in motion is under a constant force, is it true that the kinetics of the situation dictate that as the velocity of molecular friction resists the momentum of the shear component, an intolerable vector develops in a semi-rigid medium?

Stumped

Dear Stumped—
   Only on Tuesdays.

.   .   .

Dear George—
   My husband refuses to take care of the house repairs, so I have this problem with repairmen. Whenever I call one they come late, charge too much, drop cigar ashes on the floor and never fix anything right. How do you handle these kind of guys?

Fed Up

(I can't answer this letter, this sounds like a real problem. I don't answer real problems. If I'm going to solve real problems, I want more money. Come to think of it, I want more money even if I don't solve real problems. Maybe I should talk to my publisher about this, but that might create a problem neither of us could solve.)

END OF CHAPTER

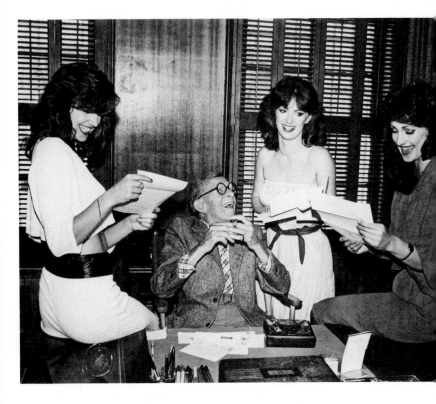

Nothing can be that funny.

5

Short Letters With Short Answers

Dear George—

My husband and I are senior citizens and we still care about each other. Is it okay to make love in the 90s?

Getting Up There

Dear Getting—

I think it's best around 70 or 75. If it gets any hotter than that, I turn on the air conditioner.

.   .   .

Dear George—

I am a Senior Citizen, and they tell me I should be enjoying the Golden Years. How can I awake every morning with a song in my heart?

Still Kicking

Dear Still—

Try an AM-FM pacemaker.

Dear George—

Has Dean Martin really done as much drinking during his career as he says?

An Imbiber

Dear Imbiber—

Let me put it this way. If Dean Martin were to apply for a job as a professional wine taster, he would be considered overqualified.

(So Dean drinks a little. But don't forget—he never drinks when he's not working.)

Dear George—

If you had your choice, what would you have for your epitaph?

Inquisitive

Dear In—

Who cares as long as I'm standing there reading it.

(That wasn't my original answer. My first answer was a shrimp cocktail. Then my secretary explained to me, "An epitaph is not an appetizer. An epitaph is something that goes on a tombstone. How could you say a shrimp cocktail?" I said, "While I'm standing there reading my epitaph, I'd like to eat something.")

Dear George—

I'm eighteen years old, and I want a motorcycle for my birthday. But my parents say it's too dangerous. Don't you think it's about time they stopped worrying about me getting hurt? After all, it's my body—right?

Grounded

Dear Ground—

From your parents' point of view it is *not* your body, they built it before you moved in—right?

Dear George—

After being married to the same woman for 42 years I have to admit that it's starting to go stale. Oh, we still do it now and then, but it's always the same. Why is that? I know her every move before she makes it.

                                                          Bored

Dear Bored—

Look, she moves, don't complain.

(How about that guy, writing a letter like that. He's married 42 years and knows her every move. She knows his *moves, too, and I didn't get a letter from her. He ought to be ashamed of himself. I'm sorry I answered him.)*

Dear George—

My boyfriend is very romantic about our dinner dates. But every time he invites me to an expensive restaurant he insists we go Dutch. How can I break him of this habit?

Busted

Dear Busted—

The next time he invites you to go Dutch, put on a pair of wooden shoes and kick him where it hurts—in his wallet.

(That's not the world's greatest answer, but I'm still mad at that letter before this. Married 42 years and knows her every move! He's lucky somebody else doesn't know her every move. If he keeps complaining, somebody else will. I better stop getting so worked up about these things. It could keep your author up nights. Look, if I'm going to be up all night, I want a better reason.)

Dear George—

I don't understand today's kids. What do you think about young girls who date older men?

Out of Step

Dear Out—

I think about them 24 hours a day. Well, not exactly 24 hours, I need at least an hour off for my nap.

.   .   .

Dear George—

I recently read in a magazine that Wyatt Earp is buried in a Jewish cemetery in Los Angeles. George, why did they bury Wyatt Earp there?

A Fan of Earp

Dear Fan—
Because he died.

Dear George—

Three years ago I took up scuba diving, and now it's the highlight of my life. I can't get enough of it. Have you ever tried it?

Estelle

Dear Estelle—

I did, but I had to give it up. The cigar smoke kept fogging up my mask.

.   .   .

Dear George—

I keep hearing about the sexual revolution. When did it start, and is it still going on?

Potential Volunteer

Dear Potent—

I wouldn't know. The last revolution I was in was the American Revolution. And from what I saw, sex didn't play too big a part in it. But maybe I was just in the wrong bunkers.

Dear George—

Thanks a lot! I got my wife that blue convertible for her birthday last week, and she hasn't talked to me since. Now I've got to apologize, take it back and get her what she wanted in the first place.

Farley in Fairfield

Dear Farley—

That's the worst thing you can do. Don't give in. She's testing you. Deep down she wants you to be strong. It may take a while, but she'll come around. I know what I'm talking about. I read Dr. Joyce Brothers faithfully.

.　.　.

Dear George—

I just turned 50, but I enjoy dressing like a 25-year-old girl. Is this a mistake?

Fabulous at Fifty

Dear Fab—

Only if your name is Irving. Or Seymour. Or Irving Seymour.

END OF CHAPTER

I have a feeling you still think I'm making up these letters. Be honest, that's what you're thinking, right? Well, it's very upsetting.

It's difficult enough to sit around and write a book, or even stand around to write a book, without having to worry about you worrying about me worrying about you.

There, you see, I just used three worries in one sentence. That's how upset you got me. If I was thinking straight, I could have written that sentence with one worry. Making up letters—if you're going to keep thinking that, I'm going to stop writing this book.

What am I saying? I'm getting paid twice as much as I did last time. I'm going to finish this book. You think what you want, I write what I want.

....

Dear George—

Do you think a daily massage does any good?—

—*It must. They love it.*

6

Short Letters With Long Answers

Dear George—

I have a ten-dollar bet about you. My friend said you once did an act with a seal. I said there's no way a classy performer like you would have ever worked with a seal. Tell me you didn't. I'll split with you.

Wagering Wally

Dear Wagering—

I could tell you I didn't, but I'd be lying, and for five dollars it's not worth it.

When I started in vaudeville it didn't take me long to figure out that if I wanted to eat, I'd have to work with a partner. But every time I'd find myself a partner who was good, he would start looking for a partner who was good and I'd be out of work again. Then I started to look for a partner who wouldn't leave me, and I found one—a very talented seal. And we called ourselves Captain Betz & Flipper. I was Captain Betz.

Flipper wasn't bad. He'd balance a ball on his nose, walk up a ladder and he'd take a mallet in his teeth and play a xylophone. And for a finish I would balance a ball on my nose, and Flipper would smoke a cigar.

We opened at the Hippodrome in Cleveland, and after the first performance the manager came back and said, "Captain, you've got a very talented seal there, you ought to give him first bill-ing." I didn't mind him saying that, but he said it in front of the seal. It was embarrassing.

Everywhere we played, people would make comments like that. It got so I couldn't handle Flipper. Every time I'd throw him a fish he'd throw it back at me. Finally I had it with him.

Wally, you're right, a classy performer like me didn't have to work with seals. Two weeks after I dropped Flipper I opened at the Poli Theater in Wilkes-Barre with my new act, Captain Betz & Fido.

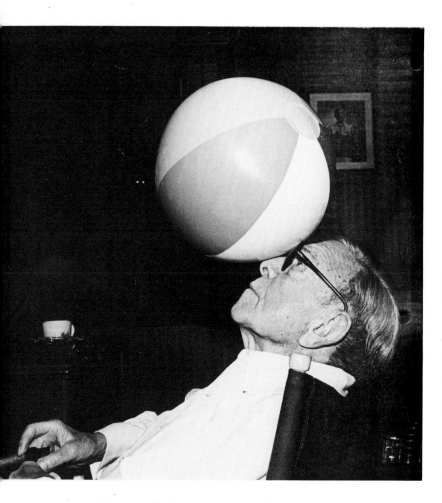

Some tricks you never forget.

Dear George—

As Henny Youngman would say—take my grandson, please! It used to be he couldn't get enough of Gramps. Now at 10 he's through with me. Nothing I have to say seems to interest the little rascal. If this is the Generation Gap, you can have it.

Disillusioned Grand Pappy

Dear D.G.P.—

Forget the Generation Gap, relax and keep talking. He needs you as much as you need him. You should be like my friend Barry Lefkowitz, who thinks he's the greatest thing that's happened to his grandson.

Last Sunday the three of us were walking in Roxbury Park, and the kid said, "Grampa, what makes the trees have leaves?" And Barry said, "What am I, a horticulturist? How would I know why trees have leaves?"

Then after a moment the kid said, "Grampa, why is that dog walking sideways?" And my friend said, "If I knew why the dog is walking sideways I'd be a veterinarian."

A few minutes later, "Grampa, why do robins eat worms?"

"Why do robins eat worms—what am I, the Birdman of Alcatraz?"

We walked a little more, and the kid said, "Grampa, could I ask you another question?"

And my friend said, "Ask, ask. How else are you gonna learn?"

(I have to be honest. That's a funny story, but it's not new. Then again, neither am I. I didn't have to tell you that's an old story. I could have said I made it up. But I don't lie. I don't say I never lied. If I never lied, I could be like George Washington, I could be President of the United States. Wait, I think I remember telling one lie. Well, Secretary of State isn't a bad job, either. That's an old line, too. Look, I'm 89, what do you want me to have—new stuff?)

Dear George—

I'm in trouble with the law and I need an attorney, but I can't afford one. Since I know that I'm innocent, I'm thinking about defending myself. Do you think this is a good idea?

On Trial in Tulsa

Dear On—

There's an old saying that anyone who defends himself has a fool for an attorney. I remember the time a friend of mine had a head-on collision with another car. He was so sloshed he was driving on the wrong side of the road. When the case went to court, my friend decided to defend himself.

The plaintiff's lawyer argued that the accident occurred because my friend had been drinking. My friend claimed that the accident was due to the fact that the other driver had NOT been drinking. He argued that if the other driver had been loaded, he, too, would have been driving on the wrong side of the road, and the two cars would have missed each other.

My friend told me this story while I was visiting him in jail.

(I just remembered, I never told you how I happened to find that seal, Flipper, that I worked with. I better tell you. It's an amusing story and it's true. That doesn't mean the other stuff I've been telling you isn't true . . . or amusing.

Anyway, this very close friend of mine, Jack Webber, who did an act with his wife, called Webber & Webber, wanted an exciting finish, so they added a seal at the end of their routine. And they were thrilled with their new finish.

But when the booker saw the act he told them to take the seal out and finish with a song and dance.

Webber said, "But the seal is a novelty. Everybody finishes with a song and dance."

And the booker said, "I know, and everybody's working but you."

And that's how I got possession of the seal. Now wasn't that worth waiting for?)

Dear George—

I am a financial consultant and have always done well on my own, but my wife has been nagging me that I should get a partner. She keeps hitting me with that old bromide that "two heads are better than one." What do you think?

Henpecked

Dear Hen—

I have never believed that two heads are better than one. When I was going to school we had a kid on the block who had two heads. His parents named him Frankie and Johnny after a song they used to dance to when they were courting. But he wasn't any smarter than the rest of us. Everything you told him would go in one ear and out the other, and in one ear and out the other.

I had a brother who thought four heads were better than one, but he had a hat store.

Look, you have to take these sayings with a grain of salt. There's another one that makes no sense. Who wants to take sayings with salt? Salt is bad for you. I don't season my sayings. If I take a saying, I may sprinkle a little sugar on it, or pepper, but never salt.

Then there's that other one: "If the shoe fits, wear it." Until I heard that one I went around for 53 years in shoes that didn't fit me. Now, thanks to that saying I'm wearing shoes that fit me, but my feet hurt from the shoes I wore before.

Well, Hen, I hope this solves your problem. If it doesn't, maybe I should get a partner, maybe two heads *are* better than one.

Dear George—

I'm trying to break into television as a comedy writer, and it's not easy. Coming up with funny stuff every week is murder. Did you have that same problem when you started out?

Struggling Novice

Dear Strug—

I started in vaudeville, and we didn't have to come up with new stuff every week. If you had a good routine, you could use it for years and years. And if anybody stole one of your jokes, it was the end of the world, either for you or for him.

Strug, let me tell you a story about how important one joke could be. It must have been fifty years ago, and Gracie and I were doing very well. We were playing the Palace Theater, and before the show I ran into a friend of mine who said, "George, I've got a great joke for you. In that hunting routine you do, have Gracie say, 'This bird flies backwards. It's not interested in where it's going, it's interested in where it's been.' "

Gracie and I did it, and it was a tremendous laugh. The next day I got a call from Fred Allen telling me I couldn't use that joke, it belonged to him. I offered him $50 for the joke, and he said no. I offered him $100, and he said no. I offered him $200, and he still said no. I couldn't offer him any more, I wasn't making any more.

But I couldn't bear to take such a big laugh out of our act. So I called John P. Medbury, a very good writer I knew in Los Angeles, and explained my problem to him. Without taking a beat, he said, "Don't have the bird fly backwards, have the bird fly upside down. In case a hunter shoots it, it falls up."

Well, we did it, and it got just as big a laugh. In fact, I sold it to Fred Allen for $300.

Good luck with your career, Strug, and since you're just starting, if you want to use that joke, go ahead, it'll only cost you $100.

(I just remembered another argument over a joke that involved John P. Medbury.

At the time, he was writing a popular joke column in the newspaper, and Gracie and I used one of the jokes from his column. It went like this: I said to Gracie, "A funny thing happened to my mother in Cleveland." And she said, "I thought you were born in Buffalo."

The next day I got a call from Jesse Block of Block & Sully, another man/woman act. He said, "George, you can't use that joke. It's our joke, it belongs to us." I said, "How can it belong to you? I got it out of Medbury's column yesterday." And Jesse said, "But we got it out of the first edition."

I also sold that to Fred Allen for $300.)

Dear George—

Our family lives here in Hollywood, and my daughter, Pearl, who is quite beautiful, has her heart set on becoming a movie star. I know it's difficult, but I read where Robert Taylor was discovered working in a gas station; Lana Turner was discovered having an ice cream soda at Schwab's; and they discovered Cary Grant advertising a restaurant by walking up and down the street on stilts. What would be the best way for my daughter to get into pictures?

Pearl's Mother

Dear Mother of Pearl—

It's very simple. Just have her get a job at a gas station, order ice cream sodas at a local drugstore and walk back and forth to work on stilts. If that doesn't work, she can always marry a producer or two.

(It's not easy getting into motion pictures. Sometimes it's not easy getting out of a picture. That was my problem.

Back in the early thirties, when Gracie and I were doing our radio show, they brought us to Hollywood to do a movie. We were very excited about it until we got the script. The opening shot had us in a rowboat in the middle of the ocean trying to hitch a ride. And there was this iceberg that split apart to let us go through. It was a very believable opening. What Gracie and I were supposed to be doing stranded in the middle of the ocean, I never understood.

I told my agent Abe Lastfogel, who was the head of the William Morris Agency at that time, that I didn't think this picture would help our career, and I'd like to get out of it. Abe said, "Look, you don't get out of a picture just like that, but we'll go talk to the producer."

The next day we did. I said, "Go ahead, Abe, tell him."

He said, "I don't know what to do, you tell him."

So I said, "Look, Mr. Harris" (that wasn't his name, but I couldn't call him Mr. Lastfogel because Abe was standing next to me). Anyway, I said, "Mr. Harris, there's no way Gracie and I can do that opening scene, it doesn't make any sense. It's unbelievable."

He said, "For Burns and Allen it's believable."

I said, "What about that scene where you've got W. C. Fields flying on a motorcycle? A motorcycle doesn't fly, W. C. Fields flies."

"Don't tell me how to make pictures," he said, "you've got a pay-or-play contract, and we'll do it my way. And I don't want to see you again until you're going through that iceberg."

Abe pulled me out of the office. I said, "Abe, you're my agent, why didn't you say something?"

He said, "What could I say?"

"I'll show you how to get out of this picture,"
I told him.

We went back into the office and I said, "Mr.
Harris, you have a beautiful big house in Bel Air."

He said, "Yes."

"And you'd like to continue to live there?"

He said, "Yes."

"Well, if you make this lousy movie, you won't.
It's the worst thing I ever read. And anyone who
will produce a movie like this knows nothing about
show business. And if you do this, you'll be laughed
right out of Hollywood!"

"No one can talk to me that way and work for
me," he said, and tore up my contract.

Abe and I left, and out in the hall, I said, "Abe,
that's the way to get out of a picture."

I don't remember the name of the movie, but it
was a very big hit.)

END OF CHAPTER

....

Dear George—
How do you deal with those pesky salespeople who constantly knock at your door?—

—*Some annoyances you just have to put up with.*

I didn't even wait for this little salesgirl to ring my bell. I bet she could, too.

7

Short Letter With Very Long Answer

Dear George—

My grandfather always keeps talking about vaudeville. Who were some of the great vaude-villians you worked with? And what can you tell me about them?

Curious Yuppie

(I've been asked this question so many times, instead of just answering it for him, I'm going to answer it for all of you.

I can't mention all the stars I've worked with, but here are just a few you might enjoy reading about:)

Ethel Barrymore was one of the famous Barry-mores, America's leading theatrical family. In the summertime she would play ten weeks of vaude-ville in a sketch called "The Twelve-Pound Look." One week she was headlining in the Albee Theater in Brooklyn, and Gracie and I went on right after her.

The old people came to see Ethel before they died; the young people came to see Ethel before Ethel died. Ethel didn't die and the old people didn't die. Gracie and I died. We couldn't follow "The Twelve-Pound Look."

Houdini was the greatest escape artist in the world. He could get out of a locked steamer trunk in thirty seconds. He went into Mae West's dressing room once and couldn't get out for two days.

The four Marx Brothers: Chico, Groucho, Zeppo and Harpo. The only way they could have been funnier was if there were five of them. Come to think of it, there was a fifth one—Gummo. But he wasn't funny. So they were funnier with four of them.

In our early days together I must have met them a dozen times, and they never remembered me. Maybe if I had changed my name to Burnso, they would have.

Eva Tanguay. They called her the "I Don't Care Girl." She did a song where she claimed she couldn't sing, she couldn't dance, she couldn't act, but she didn't care.

She was one of the top headliners. But that's show business. I was starving, couldn't get a job, and I cared. She made a fortune, and didn't care.

This is the one and only Will Rogers. It's amazing how far he got just standing on the stage, twirling a rope and talking. But that talk of his was pretty sharp. One of the things he said was that no one could be as funny as the politicians in Washington. He was wrong, he was funnier.

Sophie Tucker was billed as "The Last of the Red
Hot Mamas." She was a headliner for fifty years.
That's a long time to be a Red Hot Mama. I never
knew a mama who could stay hot for fifty years—
lukewarm, maybe, but not hot.

Here's Clayton, Jackson & Durante with Ruby Keeler. I don't remember Ruby being with them very long, but I sure remember Lou Clayton, Eddie Jackson and Jimmy Durante. What an act they had! When they brought the house down it included the scenery, the piano and anything else they could lay their hands on. They did great business, but they had to . . . to pay for everything they destroyed.

Bill "Bojangles" Robinson. I worked with him
many times. He was a great tap dancer and an
even greater showman. When he did that routine
of his dancing up and down the stairs, he always
stopped the show.

People ask me why they called him "Bojangles."
What should they have called him—Bo Derek?

A performer like Bill Robinson comes along once
in a lifetime, and I'm glad he came along during
mine.

This is an early Jack Benny. I don't know about the hair, but the violin is genuine.

That's Eddie Cantor in blackface. Cantor was one of the greatest. His biggest hit was a song called "Suzie." He sang "Suzie," but I knew Suzie. I knew Suzie better than he knew Suzie. Suzie wasn't bad, she sang in my key.

This is Mr. Berle before he became "Mr. Television." You can tell he was funny even then because his hat is turned up. But there's nothing I can say about Milton that he hasn't said about himself.

Fannie Brice was the first great stand-up comedienne. She got laughs, she sang, she danced, she took pratfalls, she could be broad, she could be subtle—and she did a great imitation of Barbra Streisand.

This is a team who worked in vaudeville for a lot of years. I think they called their act Burns & Allen. Miss Allen was a very talented comedienne. I always felt she could have done better with another guy.

W. C. Fields not only said things funny, he moved funny, he looked funny, everything he did was funny. He was funny on the stage, he was funny in the movies, he was even funny at funerals.

Gracie and I did several movies with Bill Fields. In one of them there was a scene in a café where Fields was sitting at a table with the beautiful Peggy Hopkins Joyce, and Gracie was the waitress. Toward the end of the scene, Gracie said, "After I wait on you I've got to rush right home. My sister just had a baby."

Fields asked, "Is it a boy or a girl?" and Gracie said, "I don't know. That's why I want to get home. I can't wait to find out if I'm an uncle or an aunt." And then she made her exit.

Well, Bill Fields felt he needed a laugh to top her, but nobody on the set could think of anything. So I walked over to Bill and said, "After Gracie hits you with that silly line, here's a funny thing you can do. There is a glass of water, a cup of coffee, a martini and a napkin in front of you. Why don't you take two lumps of sugar, put them in the water, stir the coffee, drink the martini and wipe Peggy Hopkins Joyce's mouth with your napkin."

Fields looked up at me and said, "Yeah. Thanks, George. This is the first time I've ever liked a straight man."

Vernon and Irene Castle. They were the top dancing team of the 1920s. They were ballroom danc-
ers, and their finale was an exciting number called
"The Castle Walk." It swept the country, everybody was doing it. Irene was a sensational dancer.
I can't say how good Vernon was, because I never
danced with him.

Al Jolson—I still think he was the world's greatest entertainer. I'll never forget a World War I bond rally. It was the biggest show ever put together. Every star you could think of was on it.

Finally, Enrico Caruso, the opera sensation of his time, came on. He sang an aria from *Pagliacci*, and then he introduced a new war song written by George M. Cohan, called "Over There." He brought the house down.

Then out came Jolson. He walked to the center of the stage, looked at the audience and said, "You ain't heard nothin' yet!" Can I tell you something, he was right.

END OF CHAPTER

....

Dear George—

Everyone's jogging these days. Would you advise it?—

—*It helps me. I do this every morning.*

8

Intriguing Letters With Provocative Answers

Dear George—

I am really looking forward to your new book. I've always loved your humor, and as a psychologist, what I appreciate even more is your straightforward, hide-nothing approach.

You admit your age, your lack of formal education, and you're the first to say that until Gracie came along you were a flop. I find this not only an endearing trait, but a very healthy one as well.

Some people are shocked by what I say, and how I say it on my radio and TV shows. I don't try to be shocking, it's the only way I can do it. I'm like you, George, I have to tell it like it is.

Dr. Ruth Westheimer

Dear Dr. Ruth—

It's true, I've always believed in telling it like it is. However, with your favorite topic, I've reached the point where I have to tell it like it was. That is, if I can remember what it was.

Dear George—

I heard that Michelangelo didn't start painting the ceiling of the Sistine Chapel until he was 70 years old. Is this true, and why did he wait so long to do it?

Artistic Alvin

Dear Art—

I happen to know all about this, because I held the ladder for him. I knew Mike very well. And it's true, Michelangelo starting painting the ceiling when he was 70 years old. He would have started sooner, but he felt it only needed one coat.

.   .   .

Dear George—

I love to play poker. But, George, I must be the worst cardplayer in the world. Last night I was dealt a hand that knocked my socks off, but I played it so bad I lost my shirt. And by the end of the night they beat the pants off me. Can you help me?

Plain Stupid

Dear Plain—

I can only help you if you wear clothes my size.

Dear George—

I have a sheep named Shirley, and I've been trying to teach her to dance. If she could, we'd be a hit in show business. I've played disco music for her, rock music, country music, even classical music, but she refuses to dance.

George, you've worked with animal acts. What advice can you give me?

Sheepish Sheldon

Dear Sheep—

I think Shirley's trying to pull the wool over your eyes. But don't give up, I can't believe that sheep won't dance. I've seen dogs that can dance. In fact, I danced with one last night.

.   .   .

Dear George—

I know you've been in show business practically all of your life and have a very wide acquaintance. One of my all-time favorites was John Barrymore. Did you know him?

Old, Old Fan

Dear Old, Old—

Did I know John Barrymore! I knew him very well. I was introduced to him by Minta Arbuckle, who was married to Fatty Arbuckle. Now Fatty Arbuckle was one of the great comedians in silent pictures. His first name was Roscoe, and they called him Fatty because he weighed about 300 pounds. He came to Hollywood as a stagehand and was discovered by Mack Sennett, who only weighed 145 pounds. He was the one who put Fatty Arbuckle in all those great comedies.

Fatty was a very good friend of Buster Keaton, who was also one of the greats. Keaton originally started in vaudeville with an act called "The Three Keatons." He worked with his mother and father. And he never smiled, he always kept that deadpan expression.

Now Keaton was a very good friend of Charlie Chaplin, who was the king of the silent pictures. At that time Charlie Chaplin was married to Lita Grey. This was before Paulette Goddard. And Lita Grey had her dresses made in a little shop on 45th St., right next door to Wienig's restaurant. And Al Jolson used to eat at Wienig's. And right above Wienig's was the Jack Mills Publishing Company. . . . So you see, I really knew John Barrymore!

(It's a good thing he didn't ask me about George Arliss. I didn't know him nearly as well as John Barrymore.)

Dear George—

I recently read an interview where you said that you can often tell right from the start if a performer is going to make it or not. Could you tell that Bob Hope was destined to become a star the first time you saw his act?

Skeptical

Dear Skept—

No, it was not until the *second* time I saw Bob Hope's act that I knew he'd become a star. The first time I saw Bob Hope's act Milton Berle was doing it.

I'm through with girls.

Dear George—

I'm from Dallas, and I'm going around with an elderly gentleman who's your age and looks exactly like you. He lives in Beverly Hills, too, and belongs to your country club. He used to phone me twice a day, now he phones me once a day. He tells me he's writing a book of silly letters. You must know him. The next time you see him at the club ask him if he's really writing that book or just trying to save the price of a phone call.

I'm so mad—not at you, at him. But you look so much like him, I'm mad at you, too! Of course, he hasn't got your sense of humor. His idea of a fun evening at Chasen's is flipping a spoon into a glass of water.

All he ever talks about is show business . . . all those stories about Al Jolson, Georgie Jessel and his best friend, Jack Benny. I'd rather watch the spoon trick again. And he's always got a cigar in his face, which really bothers me, especially when he's kissing me. And I know his heart belongs to me, but his hair belongs to Max Factor.

On second thought, I'm sure you'd be more fun than he is. Why don't we forget about him. You give me a call sometime and we'll get together.

Cathy from Dallas

Dear Cathy—

I happen to know this fellow you're talking about. In fact, I know him very well. Don't underestimate him. He's a wonderful man. He's much funnier than I am. Everything he says knocks me out. He's the funniest guy at our club. And I love his spoon trick.

Look, I know his faults better than you do. So he smokes a few cigars a day. That doesn't bother me, but then again he's never kissed me.

I'm sure that even though he's working at that book now, he's thinking of you twice a day. You really should give the old guy another chance. But I like the idea of getting together. Why don't the three of us do it sometime.

.   .   .

Dear George—

I'm sorry I bothered you, but right after I received your answer I heard from my gentleman friend. And he couldn't have been nicer. He said he'd call me twice a day, and he's going to stop smoking cigars when he kisses me. He even promised me he'd start growing his own hair. So everything is fine again, and you were right, he is funnier than you are—much funnier.

Cathy from Dallas

(You know something, I just figured it out. That's Cathy Carr, the girl I've been going with for the last four years. I know her mother and father, her whole family. I've been in her house a dozen times. How could it take me so long to figure it out? I must be losing my marbles. Maybe she is better off with the other guy.)

This is Cathy Carr from Dallas with the real George Burns.

Dear George—

I run a small market, and this lady brings in her little kid who has a new angle on shoplifting. Every time they go through the produce section I see him eating grapes, apples, peaches, everything in sight. But by the time I get to him he's already swallowed the evidence. How can I put a stop to this ripoff?

Victimized

Dear Vic—

The next time this lady and her little freeloader show up at your store, weigh the kid on the way in, and then weigh him on the way out. Charge her a flat fee for how much you figure he has eaten.

If she refuses to pay, stick your finger down his throat. If he eats your finger, add that to the original total.

Dear George—

For eighty years I've tried to live an exemplary life so that when I die I'll go to heaven. I've done the best I can, but quite honestly, it's been a little boring. I've never been married. In fact, I've never even been with a woman. Now that I'm old, I'm beginning to wonder what I've been missing, and what I have to look forward to in the afterlife. Is there sex after death?

Heaven Can Wait

Dear Heaven—

Is there sex after death? Why ask me, I'm still here. I may not be able to answer that for another 20 or 30 years. I know of some cases where there was death after sex. But that also applies to jogging, overeating and dueling.

END OF CHAPTER

....

Dear George—

I'm bald and can't get dates. Do you think a toupee would make me look better?—

—*Of course it would.*

9

Some Very Endearing Letters

Dear George—

Our Ladies' Club is holding a raffle, and I would like an autographed photo of you as first prize, if it's not too much trouble. Although maybe you could provide a dinner with you as first prize instead. Or maybe a weekend at Caesars Palace, because I know you play there a lot. But pick the weekend when Frank Sinatra is appearing there, as we are all big Frank Sinatra fans. And make sure the weekend includes tickets to Frank Sinatra's show.

On second thought, you don't have to bother sending that autographed photo of yourself.

Pauline in Portland

Dear Pauline—

Where can I buy a raffle ticket? I'd like to see Sinatra myself.

Dear George—

Next week I have to speak at a Rotary Club meeting, something I've never done before. I'd like ten minutes of surefire jokes from you. Nothing dirty, maybe a little risqué, but it has to get lots of laughs. None of your old stuff, just ten minutes of good, new, dynamite material.

Rotary Al

Dear Rot—

I only happen to have 9½ minutes of dynamite material, so I'll have to write another half minute. And if the half minute is as funny as the other 9½ minutes, I'll use it myself. Glad I could help.

Dear George—

My biggest form of entertainment is seeing your movies. I have seen every one of them. Some of them I've even seen twice. But I have one complaint. How come you never do any nude scenes in them? Come on, George, give us a nude scene.

Betty in Barstow

Dear Betty—

In *The Sunshine Boys* I appeared topless—no toupee.

In *Going in Style* I appeared bottomless—no shoes.

Sorry, kid, that's as far as I go. If I smoke my cigar without a holder on it, I catch cold.

Dear George—

I think you're the greatest. You ought to go into politics. How about running for Governor, or the Presidency, or something bigger?

Silent Citizen

Dear Si—

I'd consider walking for the Presidency, or strolling for the Presidency, or being pushed for the Presidency, but not running. I couldn't run if a bear chased me. Even if it comes to the bathroom, if I have to run, I just don't go.

Dear George—

I've seen your nightclub act, and to tell you the truth, it could be better. I think I know what it needs—riddles. You should tell riddles. Here are a couple that are surefire:

   a) How far can a dog run into the forest? (Only halfway. Then he is running out!)
   b) What position did Count Dracula play in Little League? (Batboy!)
   c) When do one and one make six? (When one is a male and one is a female.)

I know these will save your act and push you into the big rooms.

Cal from the Catskills

Dear Cal—

I have a riddle for you: What's white, all crumpled up and is about to land in the bottom of my trash basket?

You got it!

Dear George—

You and your advice. I did everything you said, and you may be happy to know that my wife has now filed for divorce. And she's taking my house, my business, the dog and everything I've got but that lousy blue convertible, which I plan to sell so I can hire a lawyer and sue you for everything *you've* got.

Farley in Westport

(There's no point in even answering a letter like that. What can you do? You're bound to run into a few cranks now and then. Their bark is worse than their bite. Still, I don't want him to be upset with me. I know, I'll send him an autographed photo of myself. He'll like that.)

END OF CHAPTER

....

Dear George—

I'm your age and lately I notice I'm constantly looking back. Do you find yourself doing that?—

—*I never look back.*

10

Naughty Letters With Nice Answers

Dear George—

My wife seems to prefer the same old position, whereas I like variety in bed. What's your feeling about this?

Open-minded

Dear Open—

If you like *Variety,* read *Variety.* If you don't like *Variety,* read *The Hollywood Reporter.* And you can read them sitting up or lying down.

(I know that's not the answer he wanted. How do you answer a letter like that? That's a dirty letter. I don't answer dirty letters. I read them, I enjoy them, but I don't answer them. If you put dirty things on paper, you can get sued, unless you're a canary.)

Shocking! Anyone who would write a letter like this should be ashamed of himself.

Dear George—

I have been reading and hearing a lot about the G-Spot and how excited it makes you feel. I've asked all my friends about it, but so far none of us have been able to find it.

Searching

Dear Searching—

Don't ask me. I never touch anything unless it's in my key.

(Imagine asking me about finding a G-Spot. Although I did get excited once when I found a ten-spot in the men's room of the Earle Theater in Philadelphia.)

Dear George—

You've been around for a while. Where can I find Spanish Fly?

Ready for Fun

Dear Ready—

That's easy. I'll tell you where to find a Spanish fly—on Julio Iglesias' pants.

(After I wrote that answer my secretary explained to me what Spanish Fly is and what it does for you. I got so excited I gave her a raise. It wasn't much of a raise, but look, it's the best I could do.)

Dear George—

I've been thinking about joining a sperm bank. Which one do you recommend?

Ben from Altoona

Dear Ben—

One that doesn't have a drive-thru window.

.   .   .

Dear George—

Every time my boyfriend takes me to a movie, all he wants to do is fool around in the balcony. I never get to watch the movie.

Cheated

Dear Cheated—

Don't worry. They're not doing anything up there on the screen that you're not doing in the balcony.

END OF CHAPTER

Dear George—

We're all enthused here at Putnam's. This one can't miss. My secretary read the last batch you sent in three days ago and she's still laughing.

There's just one thing. I hesitate to even mention it. But I have this nagging feeling that you've been making up a lot of those letters. I'd hate to think you'd do a thing like that.

Phyllis

Dear Phyllis—

I'd hate to think so, too.

....

Dear George—
    Are you really a country singer?—

—That ain't Willie Nelson, partner.

11

Naughty Letters With Naughty Answers and Nice Letters With Naughty Answers

Dear George—

It's the dead of winter and I'm sitting in my home in Juneau, Alaska, watching it snow. I know I'm supposed to learn something from everything that happens in my life, but what is there to learn about yet another snowstorm?

Snowbound

Dear Snow—

Let me answer you this way. When I was in vaudeville I knew a stripper who worked at the Globe Theater in Atlantic City. One winter night we were having supper together, and she said to me, "The way I see it, sex is like a snowstorm. You never know how much you're going to get, how long it's going to last, or how you're going to get out of it." She also said, "Sex can't hurt you if you don't inhale," and lots of other things I can't repeat. But it doesn't matter, because they have nothing to do with snow.

Dear George—

My business takes me out of town two or three weeks a month. I'm a married man, but being away so much I am constantly cheating with other women. However, when I return home I'm much thinner than when I went away. My wife is becoming suspicious of the way my weight keeps going up and down. What should I do?

Traveling Man

Dear Trav—

The only way to keep your weight from going up and down is for *you* to stop doing what your weight is doing.

Dear George—

I heard that if you lead an excessive sex life, it ruins your vision. Is this true?

Asking for a Friend

Dear Asking—

I'm sorry, I can't read this. The print's too small.

.   .   .

Dear George—

Is it true that a lifetime of too much sex will affect your ability to spell?

Concerned in Connecticut

Dear Kansurned—

Probablee knot.

(I'm not sure, but I think the last two letters were written by the same guy. I know the answers were written by the same guy.)

Dear George—

Every night when we go to bed my wife complains of a splitting headache. She's fine during the day, but comes the night and she gets the headache. Do you think she should see a doctor?

Frustrated in Fresno

Dear Frustrated—

Should she see a doctor??? *You* should see a doctor. Or better yet, you should seė my friend Ruby Bancroft. I don't have Ruby's number on hand, but her car is usually parked in front of the Happy Hour Motel on Sunset Blvd. You'll find the phone number on her bumper sticker.

P.S. Ruby has never had a headache in her life. Although sometimes her back hurts.

I don't know if he's giving Ruby a ticket or writing down her phone number.

Dear George—

I just read a survey that says 85% of American women have sex before they're married. Do you believe this?

Pre-Nuptial

Dear Pre—

No. But I don't believe that 85% of them have it after they're married, either.

.　　.　　.

Dear George—

I just married a wonderful girl. We're both from traditional families, so of course we abstained from making love until after the wedding. Although we both wanted children, we were planning to wait a few years. But to my surprise, my wife got pregnant on our wedding night. Is this unusual?

First-Timer

Dear First—

I guess you were just in the right place at the right time.

END OF CHAPTER

....

Dear George—

I've never tried it before, but do you think you can have fun on a double date?—

—*As long as the girls don't mind sharing.*

12

Nice Letters With Nice Answers

Dear George—

At *Cosmopolitan* we salute solid achievement. So congratulations on a career that makes Bob Hope, Laurence Olivier and Helen Hayes look like late arrivals.

At *Cosmo* we also focus on the woman's point of view. And while you have become perhaps the leading exponent of older men keeping company with young women, we wonder how you feel about the reverse situation. What pleasures would you say are in store for a woman who goes with a man half her age?

Helen Gurley Brown

Dear Helen—

I wouldn't know. I've never gone with a man half my age.

OR:

I wouldn't know, but if you know a woman twice my age who wants to find out, send her around.

Incidentally, Helen, you may be interested in the lyrics of a song I do from time to time in my stage act. It was written by Billy Rose and Fred Fisher, and goes like this:

Oh, she looks like Helen Brown
She's the best-dressed gal in town
Got the skin you love to touch
Never lets you touch it much.
Oh, she won a beauty crown
In her new red satin gown
She knocked the boys dead
When she wore red
But she looked like Helen Brown.

This song always gets a laugh on the stage. Of course, those lyrics don't apply to you, because you look great in brown, black, blue, green, yellow and plaid. But not all at the same time.

Dear George—

I'm an old-time radio fan, and one time I remember Portland asking Fred Allen if it were true that Jack Benny had a burglar alarm on his garbage can. And Fred answered, "No, because Jack Benny never threw away anything." George, you were a very close friend of Jack Benny, was he really that cheap?

Old-Timer

Dear Old—

Yes, he was that cheap. But just in real life, not on the stage. I switched that to be funny, but it's not much of a switch. I don't feel well today.

(The truth is that Jack Benny's cheapness was a made-up character for the show. And he wasn't just cheap, he was the cheapest. Back in those days radio was full of extreme characters, and that's what made them stars. Jim Backus' character "Hubert Updike" wasn't just rich, he was the richest.

If you were the poorest, it was funny . . . or the skinniest . . . or the dumbest . . . and if you had no talent, you had it made. With a little talent you were in trouble, but with no talent you were a star. It took me a while, but I finally made it.)

Dear George—

I'm a minister and a long-time fan of yours. I could use some advice on how to keep my congregation awake during my sermons. They just don't seem to be interested in what I'm saying. You're so great with an audience, I wonder if you could give me a few pointers.

Man of the Cloth

My Dear Man—

The secret of a good sermon is having a good beginning and a good ending. And having them as close together as possible.

Dear George—

It was some time ago, but I still look back with pleasure to that bit you had me do on your last TV special. What I can't get over to this day is that of all the performers on the show you not only worked the hardest, but you used the least makeup.

George, you would be shocked if you knew how often I talk about you to my elderly patients in trying to bring them out of the depression, resignation and sense of futility that besets them. Some are considerably younger than you are, but they are convinced their life is over. You're my prime example, living proof of the benefits of a positive "up" attitude, and to be able to point out your continuing activity, popularity and success is invaluable.

So you see, you can't quit now, even if you wanted to.

Dr. Joyce Brothers

Dear Dr. J.—

Comedians don't quit. If they hear one laugh, they keep going. Which is exactly what I intend to do. I'm not quitting anything. I haven't quit working. I haven't quit smoking cigars. I haven't quit drinking martinis. Actually, there is one thing I've given up. I quit that last week.

By now I'm sure everyone knows my opinions about retiring. I've talked about it on the stage

Dr. Joyce Brothers in that TV special of mine. The one in the middle is Arte Johnson. I'm not sure but I think he does have more makeup on than I have.

and in my recent books. To go into it here would mean just repeating myself, which I can't do, because that's the thing I gave up last week. You thought it was something else, didn't you? I couldn't quit *that,* it would ruin your example for those elderly patients of yours.

Dear George—

I've got a very attractive teenage daughter who has the idea that she wants to look like a movie star. Every day she makes herself up to look like a different Hollywood sex symbol. I try to discourage her. I think she should just be her own person. Since she won't listen to me, maybe she'll listen to you.

Concerned Mother

Dear Concerned—

What's wrong with her wanting to look like a Hollywood sex symbol? As long as it's Marilyn Monroe or Madonna and not Telly Savalas.

Dear George—

I'm a big fan of Carol Channing, and I understand that you and she are very close. Is it true that show business is her whole life, that she even dresses and uses the same makeup on and off the stage?

A Loyal Fan

Dear A—

It's true. Carol is always on stage. When she comes to my house and uses the powder room, she won't come out unless I applaud her. One time she was in bed fast asleep, and a burglar broke into her house. When he shined a flashlight on her face she sat up in bed and sang two choruses of "Hello, Dolly!"

I finally got her out of the powder room—and just in time.

I know diamonds are her best friend, but this is ridiculous.

Dear George—

I am so mad at the phone company I would like to reach out and "slug" someone. Ever since they split up they keep increasing local rates and lowering long-distance rates. When my girlfriend was living in Chicago I made a lot of long-distance calls. Now that she's living in town my phone bill is even higher. What would you advise me to do?

Furious

(I know you readers all expect me to tell him to have his girlfriend move back to Chicago. Well, I won't disappoint you.)

Dear Furious—

Have your girlfriend move back to Chicago.

Dear George—

I belong to a minority group that has no racial, political or social identification, but is nevertheless discriminated against. I happen to be left-handed.

At present I am in the army, and occasionally forget myself and acknowledge an officer by saluting with my left hand. For this I am constantly receiving demerits, put on latrine duty and having weekend passes revoked.

Is there some way I can call attention to this discrimination without getting myself into trouble with my commanding officer?

Southpaw

Dear South—

I would suggest that the next time you meet your commanding officer, instead of saluting, curtsy. It might get you into trouble, but it might also get you out of the army.

It's true, left-handed people have always been picked on. When you take an oath, they say, "Raise your right hand." What does that mean, that left-handed people are liars?

If you can't dance, they say you've got two left feet. If you had two right feet, could you dance any better? I've got a left foot and a right foot, but I still don't dance well. Maybe they're on the wrong side.

Even left-handed children are at a disadvantage. Whenever you see one on a merry-go-round, reaching for the brass ring, it's always on the wrong side. So the righty gets the ring, and the lefty gets dizzy.

And pantsmakers are prejudiced. They make the fly so that the opening to the vent of the zipper is located on the side where only right-handers can get to it in a hurry. What's a left-hander supposed to do, take a right-hander with him when he goes to the men's room?

Well, South, the reason I have devoted so much time to this subject is because being an actor, I live on applause, and since it takes both hands to applaud, I hate to see either hand discriminated against.

END OF CHAPTER

Dear George—

    You look great on TV. But I'm dying to know—how do you look when you get up in the morning?—

DAVID JAMES/CBS

—*Like this. But I look much better after my morning coffee.*

Dear George—

As your lawyer I have to inform you that this fellow Farley, formerly of Fairfield, now of Westport, has filed suit against you for bad and wrongful advice. I urge you not to take this lightly, as he wants both compensatory and punitive damages, and it could amount to big money. I suggest we start immediately lining up some character witnesses for you—the more the merrier.

H. Brown

P.S. He sent back your autographed picture.

13

Character Witness Letters

Dear George—

You didn't even have to ask. After all, George, we go back together to when you and Gracie first teamed up. I would have to say Gracie was one of the finest persons I ever knew. What values she had! Integrity was her middle name. If she gave her word, that was it. Gracie was totally honest. She was dependable. And she was generous to a fault.

You can count on me, George, and if there's anything else you want me to say about you, let me know.

Danny Thomas

Dear George—

Leave it to Uncle Miltie. I usually don't do courts, but I've got it worked out great.

There's no point tampering with success, so I'll open with "Good afternoon, ladies and germs." Then I say, "Let's not forget, when we talk about George Burns we're talking about a living legend. Well, a legend, anyhow." Big laugh.

Then I say, "There he is—actor, comedian, author, country singer. . . . Why shouldn't he be a country singer? He's older than most countries." Another scream. Why am I telling you? It's your line.

Then I go into my regular proven stuff. Allowing for laughs and applause, plus my entrance and closing number, "Near You," you can figure me for a smash fifty minutes.

That's a lot, but what are friends for?

Milton Berle

P.S. Have your lawyer put me on the stand last. Because as you know, I always close the show.

Dear George—

I . . . I . . . uh . . . I . . . uh just got this call from your . . . lawyer . . . asking me to write a . . . write a . . . character . . . reference for you.

Well, George, I've . . . uh . . . I've . . . uh . . . known you a good long time. I knew Gracie, too, but that's not what this is about, is it. . . .

Anyway, I'd . . . uh . . . I'd . . . uh . . . be happy to . . . write you a . . . uh . . . letter stating whatever it is your lawyer called about. Just have . . . have—— Oh, forget it. By the time I get through with this, the trial will be over.

James Stewart

Dear George—

It never ceases to amaze me, the sheer audacity of some people. Who does this guy think he is suing . . . *you?* Rest assured when the time comes, if this goes to court, I will be there alongside you. You lie if you have to, and I will swear to it.

To me, it does not affect your credibility at all that you told me "The Gambler" was a nothing song and would not sell ten copies. Feel free to call on me if you need any additional help.

Your friend,
Kenny Rogers

P.S. Now that Christopher is born and is the light of my and Marianne's life, she is no longer upset by your rather off-the-wall advice on birth control.

.   .   .

Dear George—

Sweetie, I'd do anything for you. You're a real gentleman. Of all the times you've taken me out, not once did you try to take advantage of me.

But I still think you're wonderful.

Phyllis Diller

Dear George—

I'll be happy to do whatever I can. However, I doubt that I'd be much of a character witness for you. I really don't know you that well.

Your son,
Ronnie

P.S. Your daughter, Sandy, says she has the same problem I have.

Ronnie

Sandy

Dear George—

At a time when the incidence of malpractice suits—not to mention my gorge—is rising, I must say I was not surprised to be contacted by your lawyers about your present predicament. The first inkling I had that things were not going well was when I found out that Dear Abby and Ann Landers were calling you for advice.

But be that as it may—and I doubt that it is—Jayne and I will be happy to testify on your behalf.

I personally don't really understand why you're being attacked, anyway. As long as I've known you, I've been aware that you're a stickler for accuracy. Whenever they want accuracy, they send for you and you come in and you stickle.

Steve Allen

Dear George—

You know I'd do anything for you, but you see, I no longer make movies, I try not to appear on television, I don't write books and do my best to stay out of courtrooms.

Love,
Cary Grant

Dear George—

How could I refuse to write a character reference for you?! You are one of my favorite characters!

But let's be honest! You're not an easy person to do. It's not so much what you say, but how you say it . . . and who would know that better than me!

But I love you, kid . . . even though those cigars of yours are killing me!

Rich Little

Dear George—

No, I won't testify for you. And I wish you'd stop telling everyone we're such good friends.

You Know Who

He not only didn't sign his name, but he didn't want anyone to see his face.

Dear George—

I just heard about your lawsuit, and I'm really proud to know you. Here you are, 89 years old, and you're being sued. What an honor. Some of the biggest people in the history of the world never got sued.

Adam, who said to Eve in the Garden of Eden, "What do you mean you got nothing to wear?" —never got sued.

Moses, who said to the Children of Israel, "Stop calling me Charlton!" —never got sued.

Cain, whose wife divorced him because he wasn't Abel —never got sued.

King Solomon, who said to his thousand wives, "Who hasn't got a headache?" —never got sued.

John Wilkes Booth, who said, "Sorry, I thought he was a critic" —never got sued.

I could go on and on, but of all the biggies I know, George, you're the only one being sued. My hat's off to you. And if you lose the case, I'll be the first one to congratulate you. And you can also have my hat. Love ya.

Red Buttons

Dear George—

It was great hearing from you, and I'd love to take the stand on your behalf.

The problem is, if I do it for you, then I'd have to do it for all my other friends who are being sued. Also, I might be away on location at the time of your trial. And even were I available, I've wrenched my right arm and I'm having trouble raising it, so they wouldn't take me.

Sorry, but I'll make it up to you, even if it means doing another picture together.

Walter Matthau

.   .   .

Dear George—

Your esteemed barrister enlightened me on the act of vindictive litigation by an obviously pathetic and malcontent provocateur. This scandalous and truculent attack can only be construed, by any reasonably intelligent and cognizant person, as nothing more than a lame attempt to vilify you and your age-earned unimputable reputation.

I, therefore, offer my untiring assistance in establishing the indisputable quality of your unimpeachable character to the fair jurists sitting in judgement of your suit.

Personally, George, it's not the suit that bothers me, it's your tie that's a little too loud.

Howard Cosell

Author and his cl~~o~~se friends. Author and his fri~~en~~ds.

Danny Thomas

Kenny Rogers

Milton Berle

Walter Matthau

Rich Little

Phyllis Diller

Steve Allen and Jayne Meadows

Red Buttons

Howard Cosell

Still waiting to hear from Laurence Olivier.

END OF CHAPTER

....

Dear George—
  Can weight lifting be overdone?—

—Not the way I do it.

Dear George—

You were right after all. My wife and I are back together. She loves me, she loves the blue convertible, and we're expecting our first child in May. So forget the lawsuit, and thanks for that good advice.

Farley in Fairfield

(What do you know! We have a happy ending.)

Dear Readers

Well, that's it. Now you can go back to whatever you were doing, and I can go back to my
Tuesday-night bowling.

I hope you enjoyed the book. If you did, feel
free to drop me a line, but please don't start it
"Dear George." And don't expect an answer. I'm
answered out.

At the end of every book of mine, I've always
made it a point to name all those who helped me
with it. Some authors don't do this. But I'm a firm
believer in spreading the blame. I'm generous that
way.

Let me begin the credits by mentioning Hal
Goldman, Harvey Berger, Bob O'Brien and Jay
Grossman. They're not my backup singers, they
are the accomplished, creative, imaginative and

prolific writers who contributed so much to these pages, including this line. For my part, I have to say we were a good team, and we had lots of laughs together. The chemistry couldn't have been better—the writing, maybe, but not the chemistry.

This is now Hal's fourth book with me, so he knows exactly how I think, which amazes me, because *I* don't know how I think.

For Harvey it's the third time around. It's great working with him, too, because he knows how Hal thinks. This is the first book with me for Bob and Jay, so they don't know how anybody thinks, and they don't care.

And now I come to someone who has been invaluable to me, my secretary, Jack Langdon. Jack's been with me for 26 years, and every year he's asked me for a raise. This year I'm finally giving it to him. I hope he doesn't read the book, because I want it to be a surprise.

Nothing dresses up a book like a lot of pictures. I'm sure you have noticed all those photographs of me and the four models, Sheila Aldridge, Camille Calvet, Monica Maynor and Lori Goldstein. Believe me, it's not easy taking a picture standing next to a sexy body. But the girls held up well.

While we're on pictures, I should mention the fine photographer who took most of them, Peter Borsari. In fact, he's taken hundreds of pictures of me for my last three books, so I thought I'd take one of him. Here it is:

I forgot to tell him to say cheese.

Of course I want to thank all my close show-business friends who wrote all those nice, complimentary things about my character. They may not have seemed complimentary to you, but I know my character better than you. Believe me, ladies and gentlemen, they were complimentary.

Now to my personal manager, Irving Fein. I can't say enough nice things about Irving, so I won't. Yes, I will, I changed my mind. He's bright, he's dependable, he's conscientious, he's trustworthy, he's warm, he's giving, he's nice. In fact, it's because I think so much of him that I keep working all the time. I'm not doing it for me, it's for him. I want this nice guy to keep living well.

Then there are my literary agents, Arthur and Richard Pine. I must give credit where credit is due, and despite what you read in the introduction, they were the ones who thought of the title. Arthur came up with "Dear," and Richard came up with "George." Or was it the other way around? I wouldn't want to hurt their careers.

I'd never forgive myself if I neglected to thank Phyllis Grann. She not only has a sense of what the public wants, but she has great taste. I know that, because every time she sees me, she asks, "Where do you get your shirts?"

Finally, I better thank Cathy Carr from Dallas. She really didn't have anything to do with the book, but if I don't thank her, she may not have anything to do with the author.

Well, that takes care of just about everyone except you readers, especially those of you who bought the book. If there are enough of you, I'm sure my literary agents will come up with another good idea that Phyllis Grann will try to talk me into writing. And she just might succeed. How could I turn her down, she loves my shirts. Besides, between you and me, I'm sick of bowling.

The last and most important letter—
the author's check!